My Dad, A Rock Star?

By Chris McTrustry

Illustrated by Gaston Vanzet

Pearson Australia
(a division of Pearson Australia Group Pty Ltd)
707 Collins Street, Melbourne, Victoria 3008
PO Box 23360, Melbourne, Victoria 8012
www.pearson.com.au

First published 2010 by Pearson Australia
2019 2018 2017 2016
10 9 8 7 6 5 4 3 2

Publisher: Simone Calderwood
Illustrator: Gaston Vanzet
Editor: Kirsty Hine
Designer: Jennifer Johnston
Copyright & Picture Editor: Jacqui Liggett
Project Editor: Aisling Coughlan
Production Controller: Claire Henry
Printed in Australia by the SOS Print - Media Group

ISBN 978 1 4425 2974 8

Pearson Australia Group Pty Ltd ABN 40 004 245 943

Contents

Chapter 1	The Interesting Person Project	5
Chapter 2	An Unexpected Star	9
Chapter 3	My Dad—A Very Interesting Person	13
Chapter 4	Dad's Band	17
Chapter 5	News Spreads Fast	25
Chapter 6	Lucky-Charm Tom	29
Chapter 7	A Bad Plan	32
Chapter 8	You Might Have Fun	37
Chapter 9	Show Time!	44
Chapter 10	Let's Dance!	49
Chapter 11	Back at School	53

Chapter 1

The Interesting Person Project

Tom's class had been given a special project to complete. Each student had to prepare a talk about an Interesting Person they knew.

"I don't know any interesting people," Tom said to his best friend Raf. They were sitting on a shady bench, eating their lunch in the school-yard. "Do you know any interesting people?"

"My uncle's very interesting," Raf said. "He's started his own garden make-over business. He designs and builds stuff like waterfalls and bird baths. It's pretty cool. My dad reckons he'll end up being rich."

"Yeah," Tom said. "That does sound interesting. But like I said, I don't know anyone interesting."

"What about your mum and dad?" Raf said.

Tom sighed. "Mum works at the hospital and Dad's an accountant."

"Does your mum do operations?" Raf asked. "That could be really interesting."

Tom shook his head. "She works in the office. The only operating she does is operating the photocopier."

"Uh oh," Raf said. "Here come Conner and his mates."

Conner was the King of Cool in the playground. He and his buddies delighted in teasing other kids.

"Guess who's going to have the best Interesting Person Project?" Conner boomed.

Tom and Raf looked at each other, both knowing what the answer would be.

"I'm only guessing, Conner," Raf said. "But I'd say ... you."

"You got it!" Conner smiled broadly. "My dad was an awesome footy player. Played half-forward for the Tigers."

"Conner's dad was even on TV for some of his games," added Riley, Conner's best friend. "Pretty awesome, isn't it?"

Tom and Raf nodded. "Very awesome," they said together.

Tom soon discovered that all of his classmates knew an Interesting Person. They had parents or relatives who had been sports stars or volunteers within the local community. Alannah's uncle had been a member of parliament, while Jamie's grandfather was the president of the local community garden. Rocco's mother had been on the television news after rescuing a toddler at the local swimming pool.

Tom felt like he was the only one in his class who did not know an interesting person.

"Who are you doing your project on, Tom?" Conner asked.

Tom shrugged. "I don't know yet. Too many people to choose from."

"Tom's project will be awesome," Raf said.

Tom smiled nervously. He wished he could be as confident as Raf.

Chapter 2

An Unexpected Star

Tom's dad worked for a large accounting company. He was a senior accountant and often went on interstate business trips. On some of the nights Dad was away, Mum would take Tom and his younger sister Tiffany to their grandparents for dinner.

Tom was silent during the drive to Grandma and Grandpa's house. He racked his brain trying to think of someone, anyone, he knew who was "interesting". But no-one came to mind.

"Why the long face, Tom?" Grandma asked as the family sat down for dinner.

Tom idly speared a piece of potato with his fork. "I've got this special project to do for school—about an interesting person."

"I'm pretty interesting," Grandpa said, smiling.

Grandma shushed Grandpa. "I'm sure you know lots of interesting people, Tom."

Tom shook his head. "Not like my friends," he said. "Their parents have been on TV or played sport. Conner's dad played in a footy grand final on the TV."

"I've played in a footy grand final," Grandpa said.

"Really?" Tom said.

Grandpa grinned. "Ah. Now you're interested."

"It's not that interesting, Herbert," Grandma said. She turned to Tom and Tiffany. "Your grandpa sat on the bench for more than half of the match. He barely even touched the ball."

Tom's heart sank. This project meant more than just school marks. This was a way for him to show the rest of his class how cool he was. Especially Conner.

During dessert, Tiffany told their grandparents about her pet goldfish and their attempts to escape from their bowl.

"They want to escape because Tom is such an awful singer," Tiffany said at the end of her story.

"I'm a better singer than you," Tom replied.

"You're both very good singers," Mum said.

"Oh!" Grandma gasped. "I've had a thought." She patted Mum on the arm. "I suppose one could say that pop music group William was in is 'interesting'."

"**WHAT**?" Tom jumped to his feet. He turned to Mum. "Dad was in a band?"

Mum nodded.

"I didn't know! That's so cool." Tom paced the dining room. "This is perfect."

Grandpa sank low into his chair. "So does this mean you don't want to do your project about me?"

"Sorry, Grandpa," Tom said.

Chapter 3

My Dad – A Very Interesting Person

The next day at school Tom announced he had found an interesting person for his project.

"I'm doing my project about my dad," Tom told a group from his class.

"But I thought your dad was an accountant," Raf said.

"He is," Tom said.

The others looked at each other.

"Does he collect money for criminals?" asked Riley.

Some of the kids muttered, "cool".

"No!" Tom said. "He's an honest accountant."

"Boring," Conner boomed.

"But, before he was an accountant ..." Tom paused and took a deep breath. *Hello Coolness*, he thought. "... he was in a band!"

Most of the kids looked very impressed.

Conner, however, looked very unimpressed.

"Your dad was in a band?" Conner looked around at the others in the group. "As if," he smirked.

"He was," Tom pleaded.

"He was," Riley said, mimicking Tom. Then Conner and Riley laughed and swapped high-fives.

Tom couldn't believe it. They were making fun of him. They didn't believe him.

"Honest, you guys," he said. "My dad *was* in a band."

"I don't think so," Conner said.

Tom was stumped, but just for a moment. "I know." He grinned at the kids. "I'll bring in some of his band's CDs." Tom hoped his Dad's band had made some CDs.

Conner and Riley exchanged looks.

"What sort of music did his band play?" Conner asked.

"Oh? I... I, um," Tom stammered. "I'm... I'm not sure."

"What? You don't know?"

Tom shrugged. "I only found out he was in a band last night."

Now, the group didn't look so impressed.

"Well, what was the band's name?" Riley asked.

Again, Tom shrugged. "Dunno."

"You're lying," Conner said to Tom. "Your dad was never in a band."

"He was!" Tom said. He stared at them, one after the other. "And I'll prove it."

Chapter 4

Dad's Band

Tom usually loved homemade nachos for dinner, but tonight he was too nervous to enjoy it.

"What time does Dad's plane land?" he asked Mum.

"No later or earlier than when you asked fifteen minutes ago," Mum said. She smiled and glanced up at the wall clock. "He's probably on his way home now."

"I hope he brings me a present," Tiffany said.

"I'm sure he will, Sweetie," Mum said.

Tom picked at his nachos. "Why hasn't Dad ever said anything about being in a band?"

"I guess he thought you wouldn't be interested," Mum said.

"Not interested?" Tom squeaked. "Do you know how cool it is to have been in a band?"

Tiffany smiled at Mum. "It's pretty cool."

"It was only for a short time," Mum said. "And it was all long before you kids were born."

A sudden thought struck Tom—what if his dad's band wasn't successful?

"Dad's band did record some songs, didn't they?" Tom asked. "They weren't just a garage band?"

"They made four albums," Mum said. "A couple were very popular."

"Excellent!" Tom said. This project had "A plus"—and "Welcome to Coolville"—written all over it!

The moment Tom heard Dad's taxi pull up in the driveway, he hurried out into the front yard. A few minutes later, Tom wheeled Dad's luggage inside.

"Wow," Dad said as he followed Tom inside. "This is quite a welcome home."

Tom dumped Dad's things in the hallway and dashed back to the living room. "Tell me all about your band," he cried. "I want to know all about it."

"My band?" Puzzled, Dad looked at Mum.

Mum explained about Tom's project and how Grandma had mentioned that Dad had been in a band.

"Well," Dad said, sitting on the couch. "This is a pleasant surprise. I never thought you'd be interested in my musical past, Tom."

"Are you kidding?" Tom said. "My dad was in a band. That is so cool!"

"I'm so glad you're interested." Dad grinned. "I've got a few things tucked away from my days in the biz. Shall I get them?"

"Yes, please!" said Tom.

Dad headed for his study. "Do you know one of our albums earned a gold record!"

A gold record! What if Tom was able to bring that to school as part of his project? He would be the envy of the whole school!

I don't know what I was worried about, he said to himself.

Tom could hardly contain his excitement. This was probably the biggest thing to happen in his whole life. In the hallway, the study door creaked shut. Tom heard Dad heading back towards the living room.

Dad entered carrying four CDs. "Here we go!" He placed them carefully in Tom's hands.

Tom picked up the first CD and studied its cover. Five young men, dressed in white suits, barefoot on the beach and holding bunches of flowers, stared at the camera.

"Ah," Dad said, as he sat next to Tom. "That's the debut album—'Meet YourBoyfriend'."

Tom pointed at the five young men. "This is your band?" he squeaked.

Dad nodded proudly. "YourBoyfriend. That's one word. Catchy, eh?"

A ball of anxiety bounced about in Tom's stomach. "You ... you were in a boy band, Dad."

"Boy band?" Dad frowned. "We didn't really like that term, Tom." He tapped the CD cover. "Now, Leroy, the bloke on the end, was learning to play the guitar. And Malcolm, the blonde fellow beside me, he could read music." Dad nodded to himself. "So, you see, we were a bit more than *just* a singing group."

The ball of anxiety rolling in Tom's stomach started to grow, like a snowball hurtling down a mountainside. "Did you write your own songs?" he asked.

"We helped," Dad said. "We made suggestions for titles. We came up with a few hook lines, too."

Tom turned the CD over and glanced at the song list—"Forever Mine", "I'm Your Boy, Your My Girl" (he didn't point out that the title should have read "I'm Your Boy, You're My Girl") and "Missing You So Very, Very Much".

"I guess your search for an interesting person is over," Dad said, smiling.

"Um, yeah, I guess," Tom muttered.

"I'm glad I've been able to share my musical past with you," Dad said. "A lot of people put us down. Well, not just us, all boy bands. But, hey, we sold a lot of albums and made many, many people happy." He smiled to himself. "Fun times indeed."

Dad pushed the stack of CDs in front of Tom and stood up. "Any time you want, I'll be happy to talk to your class. Okay?"

"Sure, Dad." Tom forced a smile. "Thanks."

"You're very welcome." Dad winked at Mum. "This has given me an idea."

Mum smiled. "Your ideas are normally very good. What's this one?"

"Just about some things I've read in the newspaper, heard on my travels..." Dad brought a finger to his lips. "But let's keep it hush-hush for now. I'll make a couple of phone calls... to some old friends in the business."

A feeling of dread gripped Tom. "Don't go to any trouble, Dad," he said.

"It's no trouble, Tom," Dad said.

But Tom had the feeling Dad's idea would bring nothing but trouble—for him.

Chapter 5

News Spreads Fast

The next day at school, Tom told Raf all about his dad's band.

"I should never have said anything to anyone," Tom said.

"You weren't to know," Raf said. "If I found out my dad had been in a band, I would have told everyone, too."

Tom looked at Raf. "You would?"

Raf nodded. "For sure. And it's not so bad. You could always say he can't do the project because he's too busy with his accounting work."

"He can't do it?" Tom frowned, then grinned and slapped Raf on the back. "Yeah! Or I can say he can't do the project because he's been scarred by his experiences in the dog-eat-dog world of music!"

"Yeah," Raf said slowly. "Or you could just say he said 'no'."

Tom didn't mention the project or his dad's band in class. He did his work and kept to himself. At recess, as he and Raf headed towards the oval to play footy, they were stopped by Conner and Riley and their friends.

"Did you bring in the CDs from your dad's band?" Conner said.

Tom kept walking towards the football game. "No," he said. "Dad couldn't be part of my project. Too many bad memories."

"Bad memories," Conner smirked. "Yeah, right."

All of the boys laughed.

Tom stopped. "What's so funny?"

"YourBoyfriend," Riley said. "We reckon they're pretty funny."

Riley and Conner started singing "Missing You So Very, Very Much" very, very badly.

Tom could feel his face burning. "You know the song pretty well. Are you fans of my dad's band?"

The singing stopped abruptly, and Conner grabbed Tom by the shirt. "Our mums used to play that rubbish music when we were little." He shoved Tom away and turned to the others. "Used to drive me crazy."

The boys laughed again, then they slouched off towards the oval.

"How…how did you find out?" Tom called after them.

"Ever heard of the internet?" Conner pointed a lazy hand in the direction of the junior playground. "Also your sister. She's telling the whole school about it. *She* reckons it's really, really cool that your dad was in a boy band."

Chapter 6

Lucky-Charm Tom

One week later, Tom and Tiffany were helping Mum make dinner when Dad burst through the door, singing a "YourBoyfriend" song.

"Great news, everyone," he said. "I just got off the telephone with Arthur Malloy."

Tom and Tiffany shrugged at each other.

"Who?" Tom asked.

Mum appeared to be stunned. "You're joking!" she said. "He liked your idea?"

Dad nodded and smiled. "He loved it!"

"Who's Arthur Malloy?" asked Tom.

"Arthur was our manager," Dad said. "I rang him to suggest a reunion for the band."

"Oh?" Tom said. "That would be hard to organise, wouldn't it?"

"Normally, yes," Dad said. "But there's a reunion concert with a bunch of other groups from our era happening soon. And we're going to be included!"

"You're doing a concert, Dad?" Tiffany asked.

Dad nodded. "I sure am." He turned to Tom. "I reckon Tom was the lucky charm that started all of this!"

"When is the concert?" Mum asked.

"Ah," Dad said, frowning. "It's in a few weeks."

"That's not very long to rehearse," Mum said.

"No need to panic," Dad said. "Arthur says the backing band knows all of our songs. We just need to go over our dance routines."

"You're going to dance?" Tom said, shocked.

Dad twirled around on the spot. "Oh yeah!"

"This is so exciting," Tiffany squealed. "I'm telling everyone at school!"

"Again," Tom muttered to himself.

"This concert will be huge. And I mean **HUGE**," Dad said. "It's going to be wonderful!"

It won't be wonderful for all of us, thought Tom. *No way*. Once Conner and Riley—everyone—heard about the concert, Tom's cool factor rating would be sub-zero.

This was *so* bad!

Chapter 7

A Bad Plan

The reunion concert was very big news. It featured on the television and in the newspapers. The hard time Tom was being given at school was just as big—and non-stop.

"Look on the bright side," Raf said, as they walked to their bus stop after school. "Everyone at school knows who you are now. You're kind of, um, famous."

"I think the word you're looking for is *infamous.*" Tom sighed. "And that's not a good thing to be."

Conner and Riley teased Tom whenever they could. But Tom had a plan to try and stop the teasing. He told Raf about his plan that afternoon.

"No! You can't put down your own dad," Raf said. "That's wrong."

"I won't really mean it," Tom said. "I just figured 'if you can't beat them, join them'."

"Have you told your dad that Conner is hassling you?"

"No way!" Tom said. "He's really excited about the concert. He's done heaps of practice—singing and dancing. I actually think it's going to be a pretty good show."

Raf sighed. "Then tell everyone that."

"That's easy for you to say," Tom said. "You're not the one getting hassled." He didn't want to put down his dad or YourBoyfriend to Conner and Riley, but he knew if he didn't do something they'd never stop.

"And what about your project?" Raf asked. "Are you dropping your dad as your interesting person?"

Tom hadn't thought about that. He shrugged. "I'll think of something." He heard someone call out his name and turned. Tom groaned. "Oh no! Here we go again."

Conner, Riley and their mates headed towards Tom and Raf.

"They'll get tired of picking on you," Raf said.

Not soon enough, thought Tom. He took a deep breath and decided to launch into his plan.

"Hey, guys!" he called, waving Conner and Riley to join him and Raf. "I've got to tell you the latest from my dad's rehearsals."

"Oh yeah?" said Conner, suspiciously.

"It's so funny," Tom said, "watching my dad and his mates prancing about, singing those whiny, wimpy songs. I tell you, I have to bite my tongue to stop laughing. It's hilarious."

Conner and Riley laughed.

"Sick!" Conner said. "Tell us some more."

Tom shrugged. "What's to say? It's embarrassing to see …"

"Tom," interrupted Raf.

Tom ignored him and continued speaking to Conner and Riley. "Like I said, my dad's band is a joke. I know that, you know that. Everyone knows that."

Conner and Riley nodded. And smiled. And nudged each other.

"Oh, don't you reckon that's a bit rough on your dad?" Conner said.

"No way!" Tom said. "They're a wimpy band. They're not even a band. Just a bunch of daggy blokes who think they can sing and dance."

"Tom!" Raf pulled at Tom's sleeve.

Tom shrugged away from Raf's grasp. "What, Raf, what do you want?"

"Look behind you," Raf said. "Your dad's here."

"What?" Tom spun around. His dad was standing a few metres away, looking at Tom and not saying anything. "Dad?"

Sniggering, Conner and Riley walked off. Raf headed towards the bus stop.

"I...I thought you were at rehearsals," Tom said.

"I was just on my way," Dad said quietly. "I thought you might want to come along and watch. Give you something to tell your mates, but I can see you've got plenty to tell them already. Sorry to have stopped you."

Chapter 8

You Might Have Fun

Mum was surprised when Tom came home straight after school.

"Didn't you see Dad?" she asked. "He was going to take you to rehearsals."

"I saw him," Tom said. "And I sort of accidentally insulted him."

"What did you say to him?" Mum asked.

Tom told her what had happened at school. "I didn't mean it, Mum. Honest," he said. "It's just that I'm really getting hassled about Dad's band and I thought the only way to stop it was to agree with everyone."

"Sticks and stones, Tom," Mum said. "They're just words. And I think whoever teases you about your dad's band is just jealous."

"You think so?"

"I know so," Mum said. "This concert is going to be on the television. There are advertisements in the newspapers and magazines. It's a very big event."

"I owe Dad an apology, don't I?" Tom said.

"You owe him a big apology," Mum said.

After he finished his homework, Tom practised what he would say to Dad over and over. Dinner came and went and Tiffany went to bed.

"I'm heading off to bed now," Mum said, later in the evening.

Tom said goodnight. "I'm going to wait up for Dad," he added.

He dozed off on the sofa. He woke up when his dad's car pulled into the driveway. When Dad crept inside, Tom was waiting in the dark hall.

"Hi Dad," Tom said from the dark.

Dad gave a startled cry. "Oh, Tom! I thought everyone would be asleep."

"Sorry," Tom said quickly, flicking on the lights. "Sorry for scaring you. And I'm sorry for what I said about your band." He took a deep breath. "Some kids were being nasty. I wanted to be strong and stick up for you, but I couldn't." He lowered his head. "I really am proud of you."

"Thanks for being honest, Tom." Dad sighed and placed his rehearsal bag on the floor.

"How are rehearsals going?"

"Very smoothly," Dad said. "It's like we never stopped performing. The guys are back in the groove. Everything is going really well."

"That's great!" Tom said.

Doors opened upstairs and lights were turned on.

"Oh no," Tom said to Dad. "It looks like I'm in trouble again."

Mum and Tiffany appeared at the top of the stairs, rubbing sleep from their eyes.

"What's going on down there?" Mum said.

"Tom and I are just having a chat," Dad said.

"A nice chat?" Mum asked, looking at Tom.

"A very nice chat," said Dad. "I was just telling Tom about rehearsals."

"I'd like to hear about that, too," Tiffany said.

Mum and Tiffany came downstairs.

"How about I make everyone some hot chocolate?" Dad said.

"Yes, please," said Mum, Tom and Tiffany.

They all sat down with their hot chocolate and dad told them all about rehearsals.

"No problems so far," Dad said. He wagged his finger at Mum. "I told you we'd be great." He turned to Tom and Tiffany. "And kids, the other bands are just as good. It's going to be a great show."

"That's cool, Dad," Tom said, smiling. "Very cool."

"It's very exciting," Tiffany added. "I can't wait to see Dad singing and dancing."

Tom frowned. "Tiffany's going to the show?"

"You're all going," Dad said. "Cool, isn't it?"

"Yeah," Tom said, softly. "Very cool."

The next morning, Tom met Raf near their classroom.

"So, you have to go to the concert?" Raf said. He shook his head. "Man, that's mean. But then again you were pretty mean to your dad."

"I've apologised, okay?" Tom slumped against the wall. "And I know, my plan was dumb. I just didn't want to get hassled by Conner and his crew any more. Now Dad thinks I'm a fan and I'm going to the show. Front row seats, too. There's no getting out of it."

"I suppose going to the concert would be the nice thing to do," Raf said. "The right thing to do. Okay, so your dad wasn't in Greenday or Led Zeppelin or the Foo Fighters. But he was a pop star and I reckon that's a pretty big deal."

"I guess so. But YourBoyfriend?" Tom said. "Man, it's just so uncool."

"Well, unless you suddenly become sick on the night of the concert, I reckon you're going."

Tom noticed other kids walking towards the classroom. "You won't say anything to anyone, will you?" he whispered to Raf. "Please?"

"Well," Raf grinned and tilted his head to one side. "Are you willing to buy my silence?"

"Yes!" Tom hissed.

Raf laughed and slapped Tom on the back. "Don't worry, Tom. Your secret is safe with me. I won't say anything. And you never know, you might have fun."

Chapter 9

Show Time!

On the night of the concert, the whole family lined up at the front door to wish Dad luck.

"I'll look for you in the audience!" Dad said as he waved goodbye from his limousine.

After Dad had gone, Mum styled her hair and Tiffany dressed in fancy clothes. Tom put on his best jeans, his favourite T-shirt and a black hoodie.

"Oh, you're not wearing that hoodie, are you?" Mum said, as they got into the car.

"I'm cold," Tom said. "I need to keep warm."

"You're not hiding, are you?" Mum asked with a mischievous grin.

"No!" Tom protested. "I'm ... I'm just staying warm."

The concert hall was a large venue and a huge crowd of people surrounded it. Everyone seemed happy—laughing, talking, singing.

"This is so exciting," Tiffany said as the family squeezed their way inside the hall.

Just as they were about to enter, Tiffany said she was busting to go to the toilet. Mum told Tom that she would have to take her. She told him to "stay put" near the entrance, and they hurried off.

Tom pulled the hoodie over his head and leaned against a wall. *I'm just going to mind my own business,* he said to himself. But something in the crowd caught his attention. He leaned to one side and peered through the crowd.

"Wow," he muttered. It was a picture of his Dad from his YourBoyfriend days—on a T-shirt.

The lady wearing the T-shirt noticed Tom. She looked down at the picture. "This is an original," she said, proudly. "From when the group was really famous."

"That's my dad," Tom said. He'd blurted it out before he had time to think.

"Is he really?" the lady said. She sounded impressed.

"Yeah." Tom nodded. "He's really looking forward to the show."

"Oh, so am I," the lady said. She pointed to a group of ladies buying posters and CDs. "We all are."

"Are you all fans?" Tom asked.

"Big time," the lady giggled. "My name's Jill."

Tom introduced himself and they shook hands.

"Is Billy really your dad?" asked Jill.

Billy? thought Tom. It sounded strange. His dad had always been William or Dad. Billy sounded like a foreign name. The name of some other person, from some other time. "Oh yeah," Tom said. "He's my dad."

"You must be proud," Jill said.

"I am," Tom said. "I'm very proud."

"Girls," she called, waving to her friends to join them. "This young man is Billy's son."

All of the ladies seemed very impressed.

"Oh, you can tell," one of the ladies said. "The same shade of blue eyes."

"And he has Billy's nose," said another lady.

Tom couldn't believe it! "So all of you like my dad's band?"

"Oh yes!" the ladies chorused. Each of them told Tom how the music of YourBoyfriend had helped them through hard times, sad times—and had made their lives happier.

"The music reminds us of when we were younger. Sillier." Jill laughed. "Your father's music is a big part of our lives."

Chapter 10

Let's Dance!

Suddenly, there was an announcement that the show would be starting very soon.

"It must seem silly," one of the ladies said to Tom, "to see women of our age acting so starstruck."

"No way. I reckon it's cool," Tom said. "Once you're a fan, you're always a fan. No matter what your age."

"I hope you can let your dad know how thrilled we all are to see the band again," Jill said. "It's very special."

"Tom!"

Tom peered through the crowd. He saw Tiffany and his mum pushing their way towards him.

"That's my sister and my mum," Tom told the ladies.

"How lucky are *you* to be married to Billy!" gushed Jill to Mum.

Mum smiled. "Let's go, Tom and Tiffany!" She grabbed their hands and they moved off towards the entrance. "Dad's going to be singing soon!"

"It was very nice to meet you," Jill called after them.

"And it was nice to meet all of you, too." Tom smiled at the ladies. "I hope you enjoy the show."

"We will," the ladies said happily.

Tiffany tugged harder on Tom's hand. "Come on, Tom," she said. "I don't want to miss anything."

"Me either," said Tom. And he meant it. He didn't want to miss a moment of YourBoyfriend.

The concert hall was packed. Spotlights swept over the crowd as Tiffany lead Tom to their seats at the front of the stage.

"I can't believe how many people are here," Tom said. He had to shout to be heard.

The houselights dimmed and the opening bars of "I'm Your Boy, Your My Girl" filled the venue. The stage lights burst into life and YourBoyfriend danced onto the stage. The audience exploded with clapping, cheers and screams…lots of screams.

By the end of YourBoyfriend's second song, fans had left their seats and were dancing in front of the stage, in the aisles and on their seats! Tom, Tiffany and Mum joined in too, waving at Dad and cheering as loud as the biggest fans of YourBoyfriend.

But before too long, the show was over. YourBoyfriend took their final bows and left the stage.

Looking around at the fans applauding and laughing—some were crying—Tom had never felt so proud of his dad.

Chapter 11
Back at School

"Okay everyone, it's time for Tom's Interesting Person Project," Mr Nguyen said to Tom's class.

Tom poked his head around the classroom door and gave Mr Nguyen the thumbs-up sign. "We're ready when you are, Mr Nguyen."

"Thanks, Tom." Mr Nguyen turned to the class. "Everyone pay attention."

Tom moved a little further into the class. "The subject of my project is my dad. Not so long ago, he was in a very successful singing group called YourBoyfriend."

Some of laughter burst from the class. Mr Nguyen stared at Conner.

"I laughed too," Tom said. "At first. A boy band, yuck. Right? But when my dad and his friends reformed for a special concert, I saw how much practice and skill they each put in. And I met their fans. I saw how much the fans enjoyed the music. I saw how YourBoyfriend's songs made them happy, brought back good memories.

"I saw how much fun Dad and his friends had singing and dancing. And I was really proud of him." Tom stepped further into the classroom. "And I think that fun and music should be shared with everyone.

"So, ladies and gentlemen—and Mr Nguyen—please give a big cheer for YourBoyfriend!"

The class gasped as YourBoyfriend swept into the classroom. Conner and Riley laughed, but the rest of the class cheered and clapped as YourBoyfriend started singing. They sang three songs. Soon all of the classes close to Tom's classroom came in to watch. Students were dancing in the corridor. Even Mr Nguyen bopped along for a couple of songs.

After their final song, YourBoyfriend bowed, thanked everyone and left.

Tom stood before his class. "I hope everyone enjoyed my dad's band. But now I know that an interesting person doesn't have to be a footy player or a pop star. An interesting person makes your world interesting by being interested in you and what you do. And that's just what my dad does. He helps make my world interesting every day."